The Bad News First

Poems by Howie Good

Kung Fu Treachery Press
Rancho Cucamonga, CA

Copyright (c) Howie Good, 2021
First Edition 1 3 5 7 9 10 8 6 4 2
ISBN: 978-1-952411-58-8
LCCN: 2021932848

Cover image: *Fleeing the Large Future* by Bob Heman
Author photo: Howie Good
All rights reserved. No part of this publication may be reproduced or transmitted in any form or by any means, electronic or mechanical, including photocopying, recording or by info retrieval system, without prior written permission from the author.

Acknowledgments:

The author wishes to thank the editors of the following journals in which some of the poems in this volume originally appeared, occasionally in somewhat different form: *Thimble Literary Magazine; Live Nude Poems; Microfiction Monday; The Big Windows Review: Boston Literary Magazine: The Voices Project; A Story in 100 Words; All the Sins; misery tourism; What Rough Beast; former people; City. River. Tree.; Club Plum; right hand pointing; The Daily Drunk; Beatnik Cowboy*; and *As It Ought to Be.*

TABLE OF CONTENTS

Love Was Infinitely Shining / 1

Lonely Planet / 2

It's Your Funeral / 3

How's Things? / 4

A Joke Is a Just Joke (Except When It Isn't) / 5

Rainy Day Woman / 6

Well, Well, Well / 7

My American Dream / 8

Past Is Prologue / 9

Elephants v. Sharks / 10

Myths of the Near Future / 11

Under the Sign of the Rat / 12

Another Word for Dystopia / 13

Broken Highway / 14

Fast Food Nation / 15

The View from Here / 16

A Poverty of Love / 17

Honey in the Rock / 18

Beautiful on a Gray Day / 20

The Year of / 21

Asynchronous / 22

Famous Long Ago / 23

From the Gallows / 25

At the End of My Rope / 27

Mourning Becomes the Law / 28

The Art of Getting Lost / 29

Church and State / 30

Bulletproof / 31

The House of Dead Leaves / 32

Heart Sounds / 33

Claw / 34

Apostasy / 35

Death Be Not Proud / 36

The Bad News First / 37

Reign of Terror / 38

Letters to God / 39

A Brush with Death / 40

Notes on an Investigation / 41

Mad Love / 42

Edvard Munch: Self-Portrait in Hell / 43

At Eternity's Gate / 44

The Third Reich of Dreams / 45

Messiah / 47

Birds of New England / 48

A Royal Screwing / 49

The Elements of a Crime / 50

The Rigorous Sadness of Erik Satie / 51

We will leave this world as stupid and as wicked as we found it when we arrived.

– Voltaire

Love Was Infinitely Shining

He arrived on the armored train Amerika with his usual contingent of generals, yes-men, and Hummel figurines. The local constabulary were tossing grenades into cellars where suspected deviants were cowering. Some townspeople had donned papier-mâché heads of party notables for his visit, but the height of spectacle came later, when the town's entire population of feral children was paraded past him in chains. My wife and I were sitting at the bakery having an afternoon coffee. From the way she was looking at me, I could tell what she was thinking. She was thinking, "Everything is alive, albeit quiveringly so."

Lonely Planet

Sometime after midnight I stepped into a smoky cellar bar, gave the miserable clientele the once-over, and located an empty stool toward the back. The bartender, a cigarette between his lips, was drying glasses with a dirty rag. In my beret and belted black raincoat, I might have been taken for a fugitive Trotskyite – or perhaps the assassin sent to execute him. A woman slipped onto the next stool. She had a face like that of a 13-year-old girl who died of heart failure following prolonged laughter. "I am here to entertain you," she said, "but only during my shift."

It's Your Funeral

The cemetery was located next to a busy landfill. You could stand at the graveside and see in the middle distance bulldozers crawling like insects over mountains of waste. No one remarked on the irony. She was buried forthwith in a simple pine coffin, as tradition insists. I am embarrassed that I sobbed too much, but that's the sort of person I am, a roiling ultra-hot cloud of atoms. Preserve me from the people who eat the same lunch every day or who cross the street to stay away from strangers. The trip seems longer every time they make it.

How's Things?

It felt as though I was under anesthesia. I couldn't find words. One morning I couldn't even recall "toothbrush," but said, "You know, the thing that makes your teeth clean." Later that week, a mural of "everyday heroes" – a nurse, a firefighter, a police officer – appeared overnight on the wall of an abandoned factory. The painting was so clumsily executed they looked like they were engaging in cunnilingus. I don't know who could have done it. Anybody. That is what caused the trouble. Police were looking all over. Kindly take my shoes off. There is a what-you-call-it (handcuff?) on them.

A Joke Is a Just Joke (Except When It Isn't)

I kept seeing the oddest things out of the corner of my eye – Nazi salutes, flying saucers, ruins. Oh, no big deal, I tried to tell myself. The truth is, it was confusing and a little scary. Turning up Main, I saw cops in battlefield gear stationed at intervals along the street. They were clicking the safeties on their machine guns off and on while inspecting the passers-by. One officer had stopped a student for questioning. "Why are noses broken on Egyptian statues?" I heard him ask. There's just too much that's hidden and unknowable, even by a person of my education.

Rainy Day Woman

She was sitting on the edge of the bed, crying and feeling "something's wrong, I should be asking for help," but she couldn't remember who or what she should be asking. Everything in her brain was white static. Secretly she wanted to see beautiful color, a purple that vibrates at the very end of the spectrum. Anyone observing her would have probably concluded she would never get away – away from clock faces with Roman numerals, the tyranny of structure, all those people going about their day on a busy street. When something needs water, you water it, you don't just hope for rain.

Well, Well, Well

God arrived on the 5:15 train. I met him at the station. His hollow-cheeked face faintly resembled Julius Caesar's. As I drove him downtown to a transient hotel, he seemed absorbed in his own thoughts. He stared morosely out the window at the approaching skyline. "That abominable steeple," he muttered as a popular church came into view. I had read somewhere that he sought out quarrels, enjoyed indulging in the casual violence of a fascist thug, but he didn't seem particularly belligerent or vicious, just tired and sad. He acted, if anything, like he didn't believe he ought to exist.

My American Dream

My old grandmother is being forced by a mob to climb a tree and chirp like a bird, and there's nothing I can do to stop it. I've already been expelled from my job and apartment and required to register with the police. People like me are forbidden to go to the cinema or theater or even sit on a park bench. Any moment now an officer will stick a gun in my face and order me to strip naked and crawl on all fours across the grass. Children will point and laugh. Grown-ups will struggle to get a better view.

Past Is Prologue

Paris, January 6, 1938. Samuel Beckett was returning from the cinema that night when he was accosted by a tramp, who stabbed him in the chest, just missing his heart. He wasn't quite the same afterwards. Maps needed to be redrawn. I'm beginning to understand something about it. The ocean feels a little sick right now. Two teenage boys beat a homeless man to death in the park with their skateboards. Stop talking and look up. Ladders cross the blue sky in a wheel of fire.

Elephants v. Sharks

In memory of Pete Winslow (1935-1972)

The seven hills upon which Rome was built have since sunk beneath the accumulated weight of civilization. Surveillance drones, security cameras, spyware – all operate without conscience around the clock. Even so, elephants in India are drinking wine and passing out in tea gardens. I once read somewhere that Van Gogh, during one of his notorious manic episodes, ate a two-ounce tube of Ultramarine Blue paint. No one thought to ask him what it tasted like, but if someone had, he might have said it tasted just like "a daisy in the memory of a shark."

Myths of the Near Future

Black-winged angels circle overhead like birds of prey. The last surviving shul is being converted to use as a tool shed. Out front a noose has been looped around the neck of a statue of Anne Frank. We're approaching the hour when torturers report in for the night shift. Meanwhile, some two thousand women and girls rally in the park against menstruation despite the ashes whirling down in gusts. Young soldiers accompanied by snarling German shepherds patrol the crowd. The soldiers are forbidden on pain of death to make friends with the dogs.

Under the Sign of the Rat

We keep our windows closed, muting the chatter of the workers building a tower of human skulls outside. A constellation in the lower right corner of the sky last night resembled a rat grasping a slice of pizza. The sky is clear and blue for now, no planes or clouds, but just one slight misstep and the air would boil and the horizon fracture. Everyone watches everyone else as if driven by an insatiable desire to report wrongdoing. The little boy kneeling at the curb pokes a stick into the man lying motionless on his back in the gutter.

Another Word for Dystopia

They kicked in the door. Your wife screamed. A few of them were wearing white lab coats as if they were doctors. The world was behaving in ways you wouldn't have believed possible just a short while ago. With a "doctor" on each side, and the people in neighboring apartments covertly watching, you were hustled down the stairs and across the street and into an ambulance. To this day, no one will talk about what might have become of you. Everything is either too hot or too cold; nothing is soft. Prepubescent girls have dreams eight feet high and made of steel.

Broken Highway

Forget God and religion, what the skinny Buddha is called. Follow the broken highway, and when you do, the only witness against you will be the flamboyant bird of the desert. You'll pass through red nights and long white days and have a guarantee of a chance to win one of 1,000 prizes – everything from a string of fairy lights to an ear in a folded piece of paper on which someone has printed, "Take it, it will be useful." Even so, your identity will remain a secret, as there's no word yet in English for a parent who's lost a child.

Fast Food Nation

Corporate-sponsored astronauts are about to touch down in the parking lot of Burger King. The coyotes and crows that usually raid the dumpsters out back fulminate against the imposition. When the land is sick, as the saying goes, the people are sick. The mixed crew of hormonal teenagers and desiccated seniors has retreated to the manager's office behind the deep fryers. They are divvying up the day's receipts while the manager, bound and gagged, groans in the corner. Later, a crowd of the curious will gather across the street, ask: How? Why? When? What for? The moon will rise regardless, a booger rolled into a ball.

The View from Here

I'm dusting the indoor plants when the doorbell rings. It's you, and you're bleeding from an ear. "What happened to your ear?" I ask. You touch it. Your fingers come away with blood. "Steely Dan on the headphones," you say. I don't move, don't even nod. Now that an estimated 150 species go extinct every day, I try not to rush through my days. And if, as sometimes happens, it feels like everything is speeding up, I'll lie down on the floor and stare at the ceiling or out the window, my view a small thing but my own.

A Poverty of Love

The guests looked on in bewilderment as my future parents exchanged wedding vows in what sounded like a foreign language. Afterwards at the reception, a farmer sang about his favorite crop and then it was the best man's turn to speak. He had barely begun when my father interjected, "Spare us your life philosophy." The wailing that erupted might have been especially invented for the occasion. Everything was burning. People, drapes, carpets, tablecloths – everything. In the years to come, I would pick through the blackened ruins. Haven't you ever noticed that only the poor have dirty hands?

Honey in the Rock

Inspired by the deathbed statement of mobster Dutch Schultz (1903-1935)

There are only ten of us
and there are ten million
fighting somewhere of you,
so get your onions up
and we will throw up the truce flag.

*

Yes, I will lie quiet.
Can't do another thing.
I am all through.
I don't want to holler.
Police, mamma, Helen,
turn your back to me, please.
I will settle the indictment.
Come on, open the soap buckets.
Talk to the sword.
The chimney sweeps.

*

Pardon me,
I forgot I am plaintiff
and not defendant.
I take all events into consideration.
The glove will fit what I say.

*

Did you hear me? I would hear it,
the Circuit Court would hear it,
and the Supreme Court might hear it.
I am sore and I am going up
and I am going to give you honey if I can.

Beautiful on a Gray Day

I had lost my job of breaking in new shoes for men with big feet, but hadn't yet found my current job of burning decommissioned pianos. With nothing much to do one day, and no money with which to do it, I snuck in the door of an exhibition of paintings by people who didn't know how to paint. The gallery walls were lined with works that appeared to have been completed by a donkey with a paintbrush attached to its tail – further proof (as if any were actually needed!) that with a prehensile tail you can do just about anything.

The Year of

Because you were watching the waves roll in, and not where you were walking, you very nearly stepped with bare feet on the rotting remains of a gull's wing, just a few straggly flight feathers still clinging to the shattered frame of hollow bones that nature had designed for soaring.

&

Sleep is the trend of the time. You introduce house plants with the intent to clear out the air and feel the chlorophyll wash over your nerves.

&

You're different now. Not bad different. Just, you know, not like 1999. You're getting older, and it's hard work and probably always will be. When you look back, you see tilted floors, a cacophony of windows, rough and unfinished spaces instead of rooms. Another "storm of the century" is coming. You can feel it. The big shaggy heads of trees seem to be nodding in agreement with whatever shit the wind happens to say.

Asynchronous

The half-starved cat that sometimes came around for a meal had become just a smear in the road. I felt sorry for everyone. For humans, for roosters, for cats. The world has got all this shit in it. It's only that that keeps me from being a total hermit.

&

The whole village must have heard it, a ripping sound overhead. Children playing out in the sun looked up. A plane was circling lower and lower. Someone might have seen the pilot's mordant smile. We'll never know. He dropped his bombs and fired his guns, and the children scattered like sparrows.

&

Autumn is in retreat, an army of emaciated, ravenous beggars. We sell weapons to both sides.

Famous Long Ago

Einstein's colleagues at the Institute of Advance Study were worried. He would sit at his desk with his eyes half-closed listening to the ticking of the universe's cooling engine. By mid-afternoon his office wastebasket would be overflowing with empty mini bottles of Tanqueray. Additionally, he had recently shaved his head and grown a wild red beard. Now he was talking about getting a neck tattoo of e=mc2.

&

Schopenhauer had a brown poodle named Atman, which is Sanskrit for self or soul. The dog would sometimes sit with its head tilted to one side and a quizzical look on its face as if entreating the philosopher to explain why he considered nonexistence so much preferable to existence. When no answer was forthcoming, the dog would get up and leave the room and deposit, like a philosophical rejoinder, a turd or two in a conspicuous spot.

&

About 600 miles south of the North Pole stands the world's northernmost statue of Lenin. The face is like a mask, with a guarded but threatening expression. More than a few

23

people have admitted to feeling uneasy in its presence. The old Bolshevik seems to be measuring them for uniforms or coffins through narrowed eyes. On the pedestal is a quote from his writings: "We're the rifles our ancestors didn't have." But, as is generally the case, irony has had the last word. The pigeons that roost and worse on the statue have the harp-shaped wings of angels.

From the Gallows

Crime scene technicians in head-to-toe white protective suits are photographing the bloodstains on planks of the boardwalk, dusting the railings for fingerprints, scooping shell casings into evidence bags. I look down from the window and think yet again about moving out of the neighborhood. Thieving seagulls with a human liking for fast food used to command the beach. It was entertaining watching them squabble over a French fry or scour the water for fish. Soon there might not even be a single living ocean left, just the creep of lugubrious shadows across the floor and up the walls.

&

Death takes such a bewildering variety of forms. A first cousin gets carried off by esophageal cancer, a childhood friend by dementia. Everyone involved, if only peripherally, feels the disturbing sensation of mounting the gallows. It's a test of some sort, must be. Just last year my condition remained unnamed. Now it has a name too foreign for me to pronounce. The doctors say my body is attacking itself, even though you can't see any outward signs yet, a rash or dark bruise. I'm often afraid, but when the end comes, oh, what dust will rise!

&

I don't know if what happened to me has happened to others. I do know I have been pissing blood ever since. Sometimes the men who tied me to the chair were trying to extract information, but sometimes they seemed to just be amusing themselves. "How is this legal?" I said through broken teeth, and the tall one replied with a grin, "It's not legal at all." Days later when I was released back into the world, there was the kind of graffiti everywhere you usually only find in a men's room – swastikas, dick drawings, and obscene references to your mom.

At the End of My Rope

. . . boys and girls from the summer Bible camp set out in canoes under a ghost moon. The river of nightmares goes winding and stumbling toward the world's grimmest-looking statue of Jesus. Word comes down that your next thought and your next and your next will require prior approval. Meanwhile, anemic vampires are rumored to be roaming the cities disguised as meter readers. Ugly gaps in the skyline grow more numerous by the day. There are UFO landings, killings by stray bullets. The only book on the only bookshelf compares heartbeats to military boots stamping on faces.

Mourning Becomes the Law

The same blue jay keeps returning to the empty bird feeder, and each time it does, our little white dog goes berserk all over again, crashing full tilt into the sliding glass door, scratching at the glass, barking so strenuously the strings on my guitar resonate. Throughout the morning, both bird and dog persist in their hopeless efforts. I can only shake my head. For us also, the world continuously cycles from light to dark, dark to light. We have the right to leave but no automatic right to arrive. One person dies every 40 seconds from suicide.

The Art of Getting Lost

Geronimo got drunk one night on mescal and fell from his horse and saw in a vision the Statue of Liberty answering a huge stone telephone. He then went stumbling off into the dawn in search of new highs. It's important to reach a stage where you don't consciously know what you're doing. No one will believe you can play the blues if you wear a suit – unless, that is, you look like you slept in it.

Church and State

Joggers, dog walkers, and couples with baby strollers slowed down when they noticed the church had fine black cracks etched all over. The expression on most faces was a combination of surprise and puzzlement. At first they weren't sure what they were seeing. But then they were like, "OK, why not?" There was a time they might have hurled projectiles at the police and passed cobblestones to one another to build barricades on a street already ablaze. Now, with daylight fading, three boys I mentally dubbed the Father, Son, and Holy Ghost just played on the carcass of a burned-out car.

Bulletproof

The relationship among spatially dislocated but simultaneous events is difficult for a lay person like me to fathom. Einstein, in illustrating the relativity of simultaneity, presumed that one observer was sitting midway on a speeding train and another was standing on a platform as the train moved past. Other physicists have since added exotic details to Einstein's illustration, such as muzzle flashes momentarily lighting up the inside of the cars. There is no mention anywhere, though, of a shooter or even of an investigator, notebook in hand, later walking the length of the train counting the bullet holes.

The House of Dead Leaves

I was writing on my laptop at the kitchen table – or, rather, struggling to – when my wife called me to the window in an urgent whisper. She pointed down into the yard. A doe, its coat only a shade or so away from gold, was feeding on the fallen leaves that blanketed the ground. My wife was enthralled, but my head was full of black static, echoes and shadows that were refusing to resolve into recognizable words. As I watched with something close to impatience, the deer went on blissfully browsing the leaves that a person who doesn't waste time trying to make poems would have raked into pyres and burned long ago.

Heart Sounds

You unbutton most of the buttons of your blouse. The doctor places a cold stethoscope against your chest. With his head cocked, he listens to the sounds of your heart. He frowns in concentration as he listens. He listens for what soon seems to you an unusually long time. You start to wonder what it is he's hearing. The dry rattle of old heartaches? The volcanic rumblings of pent-up emotions? The beats your heart skipped just last night during the exertions of lovemaking? The doctor looks you in the face, but continues listening. "Whoa," he says, "there's a lot going on in there."

Claw

There's a lump about the size of a marble under the skin of my left palm. I showed it to my brother, a doctor, when he dropped by the house. He felt the lump, pressed it, asked me if it hurt. He said I had something called Dupuytren's Contracture. As I age, my fingers will contract inwards. Eventually my hand will turn into a kind of useless claw. I won't be able to put my hand in my pocket anymore or pick up a coffee cup with it or cup her breast. I'll have to learn to grasp at straws with just one hand.

Apostasy

I don't care what the police say. I was willing to wear a wire and set Scoutmasters up. I didn't want theory. I wanted a mission. I worked with numbers, trying to figure out the mathematics that went into medieval cathedrals, but I never could. I was scarecrow thin and often freezing, and without realizing it I was moving away rather than moving toward something. I can't be sure if I'll ever return. There are times I find myself staring at the back of people's heads on the bus with just so much gratitude.

Death Be Not Proud

Inspired by accounts of near death experiences posted at Buzzfeed 1/4/2021

They told me I was dead for three minutes. I got hit by a car. There was a nice, dark nothingness, which felt kind of cozy, but I also knew it was the end, so I'd better not. Like, I wasn't supposed to be enjoying it, because if I embraced it too much, I would die. I looked up, and there was a bright light with a hand poking out making the "come here" gesture. I walked toward it and started hearing loud clanging and woke in the hospital. They told me I almost died. I said, "Oh yeah?" They explained a bunch of stuff and then offered me a grilled cheese. I had Doritos, too.

The Bad News First

Every morning there were dumpsters full of newborn babies. Every evening there was one brown shoe at the side of the road – with, some said, a foot still in it, tapping. I developed a theory that we were all just the debris of a distant explosion. By then I knew no one was coming to save me. Even the letter carrier would regularly ask for proof I was who I was before handing over my mail. As I took my driver's license out of my wallet, little white spiders would fall from somewhere and melt like snowflakes in her hair.

Reign of Terror

When the reign of terror begins in earnest, a street poet with hollow cheeks and large feverish eyes will sit at the anchor desk delivering the news in a toothless mumble and then ignore increasingly frantic signals and pleas to go to commercial break and instead recite between pulls on a bottle a long, rambling, incendiary poem, his voice rising and falling like a medieval executioner's double-sided axe, until all the baskets are filled with the heads of our namesakes and the only sound that is still worth heeding is the disputatious sound of the children's orchestra tuning up.

Letters to God

As you might expect, I get a great deal of mail. The majority comes from people pleading for special favors. They plead for a cure for their hemorrhoids, for loans without collateral, for the return of lost love. Others just want to know why. Why car bombings? Why famine? Why birth defects? Why, why, why. Sometimes children send bright, messy crayon drawings. In this one, I am looking down from fluffy clouds on a stick figure family, while in that one, I am flying like a caped superhero, the ground below inexplicably defined by orange tiger stripes. I never reply. Never. It would ruin my reputational standing.

A Brush with Death

The streetlights came on just as I was starting off for your place. I admit I may have had one glass of wine too many to prepare myself. On the walk over, I rehearsed what I was going to say. The angel of death, eccentrically dressed in the short blue jacket of a Parisian street sweeper, greeted me at the door with a wide grin. I know I probably shouldn't compare, but Van Gogh also had eighteen teeth pulled.

Notes on an Investigation

Ludwig Wittgenstein was so noisy while splashing around in the tub upstairs – part of his lifelong investigation into the fluid possibilities of language – that he couldn't hear his old friend, Professor Einstein, pounding on the front door. They were going to miss a campus talk on the metaphysical implications of black holes if Wittgenstein didn't hurry. Einstein had been looking forward all week to the lecture. As the minutes slipped away, he began impatiently pelting the bathroom window with pebbles, though he knew in his heart this was useless. It was as if the real world were small, way too small for anyone to notice.

Mad Love

You're the equivalent in French to "a crime gorgeously lit by big arched windows," why street level drug dealers are now conniving to work their way up to roof level. Soon towns and even mid-sized cities are going to be petitioning to be renamed for you. A headline says Johnny Depp Is Radioactive, but how many people besides you know an isotope when they see one or that puddles are the autographs of rain? If you were a month, you'd be a torrential August. There are rose-choked paths winding through you where day feels like night and the rain that shakes the petals loose shakes me.

Edvard Munch: Self-Portrait in Hell

He was convinced, as usual, that he was about to suffer a complete breakdown. The day's work had begun badly and gotten worse with each additional brush stroke. He squinted at the muddled canvas on the easel as though it were someone else's, the fantastical product of a stranger's delirium. The street outside his window was turning red and black. He tilted his head to the right, the left, the right again, trying to view his painting in progress from the most forgiving angle. There was a moment when what he couldn't express in words or figurative gestures he might have in a scream, and then the moment passed.

At Eternity's Gate

A man arrives on a train to visit his father at a sanatorium. The doctor at the sanatorium says the father has died, but the man glimpses his father being led away down the hall by an attendant. The father is barefoot. His hands are bound behind him with wire. The man is too startled to intervene. Meanwhile, the doctor has climbed into bed next to a patient and fallen asleep. The man somehow knows he must catch the next train back to the city if he isn't to become trapped in the sanatorium. Hurrying toward the station, he sees the corpse of his father hanging from a lamppost, a savage pack of dogs standing guard over the body. A train whistle blows. The man realizes with a pang that the train has left without him. Time is decomposing. One townsperson in six hasn't noticed or doesn't care. There is no night, no day, just twilight.

The Third Reich of Dreams

It was snowing. Because the Germans didn't give them water, the women who were packed together in the roofless boxcars collected the snow to drink. When any woman fell asleep standing – there was no room to sit or lie down – none of the others would steal the snow that accumulated on her. That snow belonged to her. On a train bound to nowhere you know where you are.

&

For the first time in decades, ducks were seen swimming in the fountains, and dolphins splashing in the canals. Hitler's former chief of staff, Rudolph Hess, 93 and the only inmate in a prison designed to hold 600, had hanged himself. One look at his death grimace, and water lilies sprouted in the prison guard's lungs.

&

The grave is now empty. His bones are gone. The faithful used to make pilgrimages to the gravesite. They would lay floral wreaths and salute his epitaph: "I dared." Police on horses tried to keep control. The blood stood in puddles in some places. But the flowers would always be back on his next birthday.

&

Politics has become interested in me. Just the other night I dreamed I was rushing across campus. I was late for a class I taught. When I entered the building where my class was held, nothing was familiar to me and I had no idea where I was. I started walking up a very long flight of stairs. The stairs grew steeper the higher I went. By the time I reached the top, I was winded and covered in sweat. Then I saw the swastika painted on the wall. I didn't know what to do. I didn't know where to hide.

Messiah

The German SS officer who had opened fire rolled the corpse over, and the girl saw the face of her teacher, with blood here and there. He had gone to fetch a ration of bread, and a loaf was sticking out of his coat. The girl drew closer. Her instinct was to grab the bread and run. Jews didn't have enough to eat. She ate inedible things, soup that was mostly water with grass, and this looked like a serious piece of bread. But she left it. Yes. She left it because she saw his face, with blood here and there

&

The shopping district was known locally as the "Street of Crocodiles." Shop windows displayed artful arrangements of dismembered heads and hands. Inside, a party atmosphere prevailed. You could find whatever you wanted – if you wanted frayed wires, metal shards, or even the revolver used to kill polymath Bruno Schulz. He was working on a novel titled *The Messiah* at the time of his assassination. Only the first sentence survives: "Mother awakened me in the morning, saying, 'Joseph, the Messiah is near, people have seen him in Sambor.'" God insists to this day that a lot that happened just sort of happened.

&

The city streets are deserted. Approaching sirens wail yoo-hoo, yoo-hoo, yoo-hoo, rattling windows, shaking the pictures on walls. At any moment the secret police could walk through your door, use a pair of handcuffs as brass knuckles. You keep waiting. There is no one to feed, nothing to feed anyone.

Birds of New England

I bought a book a couple of weeks ago at Costco called *Birds of New England*. It contains drawings of different kinds of birds – you know, wading birds, songbirds, migratory birds – and brief descriptions of their habits. What's that screechy brown bird that wants to monopolize our feeder? I look from bird to book to bird to book to bird, only to finally realize just how hopeless this is, like trying to identify a 70-year-old from his first-grade class picture.

&

At a stoplight on Mass Ave., a panhandler in a New England Patriots jersey with a rip in the shoulder shuffled up to my car. He had eyes like peeling mirrors and a knobby nose that had obviously been broken more than once. I didn't lower my window. I didn't acknowledge him. I just stared straight ahead, willing the light to change. This is how the future creeps into the present.

&

Almost a year ago now, I was sent home from the hospital just hours after surgery. The only instructions I can remember being given was to look for the tall weed whose milky white sap is said to relieve pain. And if I had to scream, to please scream silently.

A Royal Screwing

During his years of wandering from Berlin to Paris to Moscow and back again, Walter Benjamin kept a diary. "Keep your diary," he cautioned himself in an early entry, "as strictly as the authorities keep their register of aliens." In his tiny spidery handwriting he recorded dreams, Yiddishisms, profane illuminations. Paris at the time was plagued with packs of stray dogs. Returning to his pensione one night from a hashish party, he saw the dogs were actually men made dogs by their passions. He knew in that moment that all perception was distortion, a kind of phantasmagoria, the blue velvet and gilt doghouse Marie Antoinette had had built for one of her puppies.

The Elements of a Crime

One night I sleepwalked into my parents' room while they were lying in bed watching TV. "Here," I squeaked in my 9-year-old voice, "take the knife. I killed him." Then I sleepwalked back across the hall to my own bed. The next morning my mother was laughing when she told me during breakfast about what I had done, but I felt – I don't know – discredited. The fact I could act without being aware of it seriously spooked me. Still does. Every night the sky is seething with headless birds in zigzag flight.

The Rigorous Sadness of Erik Satie

He didn't permit visitors to his one-room apartment in the 27 years he lived there. After his death (from drink), the landlord let in friends and family. They discovered an inventory of cultural anarchy. The room was littered with more than 100 umbrellas. There were two grand pianos, one placed on top of the other. He had used the upper piano as storage, not only for letters, parcels, and old newspapers, but also for the kind of noises an audience would pay not to hear – sirens, taxi horns, a jack in the box. Behind the piano, they found a gray velvet suit he thought he had forgotten on a bus years ago. In the pockets were notes to himself. On one was written, "Shake like a leaf"; on another, "Be invisible for a moment."

Howie Good, Ph.D., a professor of journalism at SUNY New Paltz, is the author of more than a dozen poetry collections, including most recently *The Death Row Shuffle* (Finishing Line Press), *The Trouble with Being Born* (Ethel Micro Press), and *Gunmetal Sky* (Thirty West Publishing).

www.ingramcontent.com/pod-product-compliance
Lightning Source LLC
Chambersburg PA
CBHW030137100526
44592CB00011B/934